THE SOUTHERN COLONIES
The Quest for Prosperity 1600-1700

TITLE LIST

THE SOUTHERN COLONIES
The Quest for Prosperity 1600-1700

BY
SHEILA NELSON

MASON CREST PUBLISHERS
PHILADELPHIA

Mason Crest Publishers Inc.
370 Reed Road, Broomall, Pennsylvania 19008
(866) MCP-BOOK (toll free)
www.masoncrest.com

13 12 11 10 09 08   10 9 8 7 6 5 4 3

Library of Congress Cataloging-in-Publication Data

Nelson, Sheila.
  The Southern colonies : the quest for prosperity / by Sheila Nelson.
      p. cm. — (How America became America)
  Includes bibliographical references.
    ISBN 978-1-59084-902-6
    ISBN 978-1-59084-900-2 (series)
  1. Southern States—History—Colonial period, ca. 1600–1775—Juvenile literature. 2. Virginia—History—Colonial period, ca. 1600–1775—Juvenile literature. I. Title. II. Series.
  F212.N45 2004
  975'.02—dc22
                    2004008175

Cover and Design by Dianne Hodack.
Produced by Harding House Publishing Service, Inc.
www.hardinghousepages.com
Printed in the Hashemite Kingdom of Jordan.

CONTENTS

THE SOUTHERN COLONIES

INTRODUCTION

by Dr. Jack Rakove

Today's America is not the same geographical shape as the first American colonies—and the concept of America has evolved as well over the years.

When the thirteen original states declared their independence from Great Britain, most Americans still lived within one or two hours modern driving time from the Atlantic coast. In other words, the Continental Congress that approved the Declaration of Independence on July 4, 1776, was continental in name only. Yet American leaders like George Washington, Benjamin Franklin, and Thomas Jefferson also believed that the new nation did have a continental destiny. They expected it to stretch at least as far west as the Mississippi River, and they imagined that it could extend even further. The framers of the Federal Constitution of 1787 provided that western territories would join the Union on equal terms with the original states. In 1803, President Jefferson brought that continental vision closer to reality by purchasing the vast Louisiana Territory from France. In the 1840s, negotiations with Britain and a war with Mexico brought the United States to the Pacific Ocean.

This expansion created great opportunities, but it also brought serious costs. As Americans surged westward, they created a new economy of family farms and large plantations. But between the Ohio River and the Gulf of Mexico, expansion also brought the continued growth of plantation slavery for millions of African Americans. Political struggle over the extension of slavery west of the Mississippi was one of the major causes of the Civil War that killed hundreds of thousands of Americans in the 1860s but ended with the destruction of slavery. Creating opportunities for American farmers also meant displacing Native Americans from the lands their ancestors had occupied for centuries. The opening of the west encouraged massive immigration not only from Europe but also from Asia, as Chinese workers came to labor in the California Gold Rush and the building of the railroads.

By the end of the nineteenth century, Americans knew that their great age of territorial expansion was over. But immigration and the growth of modern industrial cities continued to change the American landscape. Now Americans moved back and forth across the continent in search of economic opportunities. African Americans left the South in massive numbers and settled in dense concentrations in the cities of the North. The United States remained a magnet for immigration, but new immigrants came increasingly from Mexico, Central America, and Asia.

Ever since the seventeenth century, expansion and migration across this vast landscape have shaped American history. These books are designed to explain how this process has worked. They tell the story of how modern America became the nation it is today.

Colonists landing in Virginia

One
SETTING THE SCENE

When the Indians stood in the shadows of the trees and watched the first European ships enter their harbors with sails like the wings of huge birds, they could not have guessed the changes that were coming to their world.

For thousands of years, the Indians had had the great land of North America all to themselves. Hundreds of Native American tribes lived in small, scattered communities across the continent. They hunted and fished and planted crops; tribes joined together into confederacies to fight other tribes. Their way of life had stayed almost the same for centuries. The coming of the white men would disrupt their civilization, and life would never be the same again.

When the Indians migrated to North America, thousands of years ago during the last Ice Age, they traveled through the frozen wastes of Siberia and across a land bridge in the Bering Strait to Alaska. The trip was a long and difficult one, and many of the germs causing deadly diseases could not survive the migration. Because so many diseases were no longer present, the people gradually lost their *immunities* to the germs that caused them.

Immunities are abilities to resist disease.

Outside James Fort

9

The arrival of the Englishmen

forest fire. Within a hundred years of Christopher Columbus's discovery of the New World, approximately 90 percent of Native Americans had died, most of them from diseases unintentionally brought by explorers. Many of the Indians who died had never seen a white person.

The **decimation** of the Native American population was a terrible tragedy. European explorers had no idea that simply by making contact with the inhabitants of the New World they were introducing germs that would wipe out whole tribes.

The Europeans sailing west across the Atlantic Ocean hoped to discover an ocean trade route to the Far East. When instead they found an entirely unknown land, the thoughts of their royal **patrons** in Europe turned immediately to hopes of gold. Spain started establishing colonies in South America and southern North America, sending home ships filled with the treasures of the New World.

England was slower to begin founding colonies. England in the sixteenth century was

Diseases carried on the ships of European explorers and colonists brought the most devastating changes to Native American civilizations. The immunities of the Natives had been lost through thousands of years of not being needed. The Native Americans had no protection against diseases like **smallpox**, measles, chicken pox, and **malaria**—to mention only a few. Sickness spread through the Native populations of the New World like an out-of-control

An early portrayal of Native people

__Smallpox__ and __malaria__ are contagious diseases. Smallpox is an acute contagious disease with fever that is caused by a poxvirus, and malaria is a disease of humans caused by parasites in the red blood cells and transmitted by the bite of mosquitoes carrying it.

__Decimation__ means the state of being reduced in number by a drastic amount.

__Patrons__ were people who used their wealth or influence to help individuals, institutions, or causes.

The manner of fishing in Virginia

filled with turmoil. Henry VIII had broken away from the Roman Catholic Church and founded the Church of England. For the next several decades, the English people struggled to cope as changing monarchs enforced their varying religious beliefs, often persecuting those who believed differently. For many years England was in no shape to worry about founding colonies.

In 1558, Elizabeth I became queen of England. Elizabeth stopped religious persecution and brought a greater stability to the country. At the same time, however, tensions were rising in the relation-

The "New World"

"New World" was to stop the spread of Spain's power. Elizabeth gave English sea captains secret permission to make raids on Spanish colonies and ambush treasure ships carrying gold back to Spain. North American colonies would give England bases from which to attack the Spanish as well as make sure Spain did not lay claim to the whole New World.

Furious at the attacks on his ships and colonies, Spain's king, Philip II, sent his *armada* of 130 ships to attack England in the summer of 1588. The faster, more maneuverable English ships, helped by a bad storm, were able to destroy most of the Spanish fleet. Only a third of the armada made it back to Spain.

ship between England and Spain. Spain helped the Irish fight a rebellion against the English. England helped the Netherlands in their fight against the Spanish. And all the time Spain was getting richer from its colonies in North and South America.

One of the early reasons England wanted to establish colonies in the

A "New World"?

White people from the United States and Europe often refer to North and South America as the "New World," while they speak of Europe as the "Old World." However, those terms are only accurate from a European perspective. Unknown to Europeans, the Americas had been settled for centuries by thriving civilizations. The Native groups already living in the Americas might just as easily speak of Europe as a "new world."

An *armada* was a fleet of warships.

Nationalism is loyalty and devotion to a country.

After the defeat of the armada, Spain became much less of a threat to England. For the next several hundred years, England's navy would dominate the oceans. England was now able to focus more of its resources on colonization efforts. Keeping Spain from expanding its territory in the Americas was still a factor, but the defeat of Spain's armada had also increased England's sense of *nationalism*. England wanted to act

An early drawing of a Native village

An Early Attempt

Sir Humphrey Gilbert, an English explorer in the service of Queen Elizabeth, founded the first English colony in the New World on the southwest coast of Newfoundland on August 5, 1583. This colony was part of a plan Gilbert had presented to the queen six years earlier, called "How Her Majesty may annoy the King of Spain." The Newfoundland harbor where Gilbert tried to found his colony was already busy with fishing boats from England, France, Spain, Portugal, and the Netherlands. The location was close to the Grand Banks, which teemed with fish. Unfortunately for Gilbert, his men were lazy and disreputable and the Newfoundland climate was harsh. It was not long before Gilbert's men deserted to the other ships in the harbor and the colony fell apart. Traveling back to England, Gilbert was killed when his ship, the *Squirrel*, went down in a storm.

on its growing idea of itself as a world power by establishing its presence in North America. Apart from this, many English people also believed in following the Bible's instruction and bringing Christianity to the Native American people.

A new land, thousands of miles from England, gave people the opportunity to start new lives. Colonies in the New World mainly attracted three kinds of English people: merchants, religious dissenters, and wealthy landowners. The merchants were looking for the wealth of the New World. They wanted gold and furs to take back to England. They were hoping to find a quick trade route through North America to the ocean on the far side beyond which they could reach the Far East. The religious dissenters were people who did not worship God in the same way as most of the people in England. Most of the dissenters who traveled to North America were Puritans who believed in a stricter version of Christianity than the Church of England. They were looking for a place where they had the freedom to worship

God as they believed. Finally, some of the wealthy landowners wanted to lay claim to the huge tracts of unclaimed land in the Americas. Many of them used the land to build large plantations where they could grow crops of tobacco or rice.

England had turned its eyes to North America, and people were beginning to come. The era of colonization in England had arrived.

Early settlers

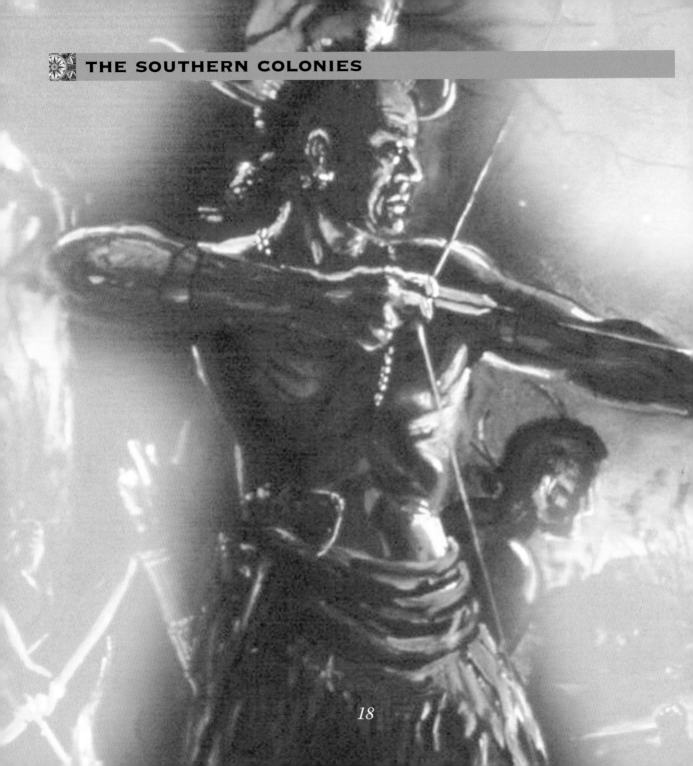

Learning from Others' Stories

History is made up of many stories. These stories often conflict with each other—but that does not mean that any of the stories are necessarily lies. It all depends on your perspective. In other words, things will look far different if you're standing in one spot from what they'd look like if you were standing somewhere else.

For example, many Americans tell stories about the early colonies that are filled with pride and bravery, the spirit of independence and freedom. Americans often honor the courage and principles of the American settlers. The earliest Americans, however, the Native people who were the first to live on this continent, have very different stories to tell. From their perspective, the years of the first European colonies were a time of tragedy, death, and loss. The arrival of the Europeans changed the Natives' lives forever. Their lands were taken from them, and their way of life was threatened. They fought bravely in their own defense, but thousands and thousands of them died.

A Dakota Indian named Luther Standing Bear wrote this about the first meeting of Natives and Europeans:

While the white people had much to teach us, we had much to teach them, and what a school could have been established upon that idea! . . . Only the white man saw nature as a "wilderness," and only to him was the land "infested" with "wild" animals and savage people. To us it was tame. Earth was bountiful and we were surrounded with the blessings of the Great Mystery.

We cannot undo the past. But we can learn from history's stories, and try to understand as many perspectives as possible.

The Lost Colony

Two
ROANOKE AND THE LOST COLONY

John White hurried through the tall trees on the island of Roanoke, impatient to see the family he had left behind in the New World three years before. It was August 18, 1590, the third birthday of White's granddaughter Virginia Dare. The last time he had seen Virginia she had been only ten days old. White expected to hear the sounds of the colony as he approached the settlement: the noise of an axe, voices, the laughter and shouts of children at play.

Instead, there was silence.

An Indian palisade

*A **palisade** is a fence made of stakes that is used for defense.*

White came through the trees and stopped short. When he had left, the settlers had been busy building houses in this clearing. Now, a high wooden **palisade** surrounded the site. Peering around the tall fence, White saw a wide empty space. Weeds and small seedlings covered the ground. But where were the houses?

White must have been very disappointed as he turned from the empty space where the colony had been. He had been so eager to see his family, since he had been gone far longer than he had intended. Unsettled relations with Spain and the attack of the

Spanish Armada had kept him from finding passage back to Roanoke. England's ships had been needed close to home.

As White looked again at the palisade, he suddenly noticed something. There, carved in the wood, was the word CROATOAN. On a nearby tree, he found the letters CRO. His heart leapt; here was a clue to what had happened to his colony. Before going back to England, he had agreed with the colonists that they would carve the name of their destination for him to find if circumstances forced them to desert the colony. If they were in danger when they left, they would also carve a Maltese cross. He saw no cross, so White guessed the colonists had traveled to Croatoan Island to the south (what is now called Hatteras Island). The Croatoan Indians had been friendly to the settlers, unlike the Indian tribes closer to Roanoke.

White intended to go and look for the colonists right away. Before he was able to make the trip, however, a hurricane blew up. White was not the captain of the ship on which he had traveled, and he did not have the authority to insist they stay to look for the colonists. The shoals along the Outer Banks were treacherous

and the captain refused to risk the ship in such a storm. White was forced to return to England without discovering what had happened to the Roanoke colonists.

Although he kept trying to come back to Virginia and find the lost colony, White was never able to raise the money to make another

Coming to America (a reenactment)

23

trip. Finding the colonists was not a priority for England, either. More than ten years went by before an expedition was even sent to look for them, and even then the men responsible for searching for the settlers did not take their jobs seriously. The colonists were never found, and John White died never knowing what had happened to his family.

The story of the Lost Colony really began six years before John White returned to Virginia to discover the settlement had vanished. In 1584, Sir Walter Raleigh, eager to begin England's colonization of the New World, sent two men, Philip Amadas and Arthur Barlowe, to look for an ideal location to establish a colony.

Amadas and Barlowe came back to England with enthusiastic descriptions of Roanoke Island, bringing with them two of the local Indians, Manteo and Wanchese. Roanoke Island was a narrow island with no hills, they said. It was located between the Outer Banks and the mainland (of what is now North Carolina), which gave it a calm harbor and protection from stormy seas. One end of the island was marshy and the other forested with tall oak trees. Plenty of wildlife lived on the land and lots of fish swam in the sound.

Raleigh was pleased with the report and went to Queen Elizabeth for approval to build a

The Lost Colony (a reenactment)

colony on Roanoke Island. Elizabeth granted the request and gave Raleigh the rights to all the land he could occupy. In honor of Elizabeth, the Virgin Queen, the land from the French colonies in the north to the Spanish colonies in the south was named Virginia.

Quickly, Raleigh put together an expedition of one hundred men to travel to Roanoke and establish a colony. The party included soldiers, tradesmen, and scholars, but no women. The

Jamestown Settlement

group arrived at Roanoke Island in the late summer of 1585. They built a fort on the northern, wooded end of the island and erected houses around the fort.

Before long, the colony started having problems. Some of the men were from the upper classes, used to having soft beds, fancy foods, and servants to do the real work. Many of the men were also from cities and not prepared for survival in the wilderness. For a while, the men behaved as though they were on a camping trip. They explored the coast to the north and south. They studied the local plants and animals. For food, they depended on the supplies they had brought with them and on the local Native tribes.

At first, relations were friendly with the Native Americans in the area. Although the Englishmen had arrived too late in the season to plant crops, the Indians showed them how to make traps to catch fish, and they traded food for metal tools, copper kettles, and glass beads. Before long, however, trouble began. A silver cup disappeared from the colony, and the colonists discovered that a Native had taken it. In a fit of rage, one of the Englishmen angrily burned the Indian village Aquascogok.

The Lost Colony (reenactment)

After that, the relationship between the colonists and the local Indians became tense. By spring, not only were the Indians no longer providing the colony with food, but they had begun to rob, and then to destroy, the fish traps. The colonists were beginning to get desperate. One member of the expedition, Sir Richard Grenville, had gone back to England in the fall to get supplies, but he had not returned, and food was getting scarce. Ralph Lane, the governor, sent groups of men to the Outer Banks to live on shellfish and watch for ships.

On June 9, 1586, Lane got a message that Sir Francis Drake was off the coast with a fleet of ships. Drake offered Lane passage back to England for the entire group, or else a ship, sailors, and supplies so they could wait for Grenville to return. Lane chose to take the ship and wait, but the ship Drake sent was blown out to sea in a storm and lost. Drake sent another ship, but this one was too big to fit in the harbor. Finally, Lane and the colonists decided to go back to England with Drake.

Not long after the Englishmen left Roanoke, first a supply ship sent by Sir Walter Raleigh arrived and then Grenville himself came with three ships. They searched for the colonists, looking up and down the coast for them. Grenville did not want to abandon the colony completely, so he left fifteen men with enough supplies to last two years and returned to England.

Although his first attempt at colonizing in the New World had obviously failed, Raleigh did not want to give up. In 1587, he organized another group of colonists. This time he included women and children in the group. One hundred and seventeen people set out for Virginia, with

John White as governor. White was an artist who had traveled to the New World as a *surveyor* with the first group of colonists. He had made many drawings of the area and the local Indians while he was there. White's pregnant daughter Eleanor Dare was also one of the group, along with her husband, Annanias Dare, and the Indian Manteo. To attract people to the party, Raleigh promised each man who agreed to go a minimum of five hundred acres of land.

The colonists traveled first to Puerto Rico and Haiti. Here, Raleigh hired Simon Fernandes, a Portuguese pilot, to take the settlers to the Chesapeake Bay to establish their new colony. On the way up the coast, the ship stopped at Roanoke to check on the fifteen men Grenville had left. There they discovered that the men had been killed by Indians.

Although Fernandes sometimes hired himself out as a pilot, he was actually a *buccaneer*. He wanted to be rid of the colonists and

Jamestown Settlement

*A **surveyor** is someone whose occupation is to determine and mark the form, extent, and position of a piece of land by taking linear and angular measurements, and by applying the principles of trigonometry and geometry.*

*A **buccaneer** was any of the pirates who preyed on Spanish ships, especially in the West Indies in the seventeenth century.*

get back to chasing Spanish ships so he ordered the party ashore at Roanoke.

Not long after arriving at Roanoke, Eleanor Dare gave birth to a baby girl and named her Virginia, after their new home. Virginia Dare was the first baby born to English parents in America. Ten days after Virginia Dare was born, John White left with Simon Fernandes to return to England for more supplies. He thought he would be able to come back right away, but it would take him three years to find a ship traveling to Virginia. He had no idea when he left that he would never see his family again.

The story of the vanished colonists—of White's return to Roanoke to find only a palisade with the word CROATOAN carved on it—is one of the oldest unsolved mysteries in American history. In 1602, Raleigh finally sent an expedition to look for the Roanoke colonists. Instead of searching in the Cape Hatteras area as Raleigh had told them to do, however, they landed at Cape Fear, approximately 170 miles to the south, and spent the entire trip gathering sassafras to sell in London. Raleigh sent another expedition the next year, but this time the party went to Delaware Bay, over 150 miles to the north, where Indians attacked and killed several of the group.

Many theories have been suggested to explain what happened to the colonists, but nobody knows for sure. Archeologists and historians are still searching Roanoke Island for clues, but they have not found any clear evidence. Certainly, nothing that would tell us for certain what happened to the English settlers John White left on the island over four hundred years ago.

Jamestown Settlement

What Happened to the Lost Colony?

Some ideas that scholars have about what might have happened to the Roanoke colonists:

- They might have been absorbed into the Croatoan tribe. The Hatteras Indians, descendants of the Croatoans, claimed in 1709 to have white ancestors. Some of the Hatteras Indians had gray eyes, a European trait.
- In the 1880s, a man named Hamilton MacMillan wrote a booklet that claimed the colonists were among the ancestors of the Pembroke Indians of southeastern North Carolina. The Pembroke Indians had European features, such as light hair and eyes, and they said their ancestors came from "Roanoke in Virginia."
- Indians may have killed them. The Indian chief Powhatan, who lived near the Chesapeake Bay, claimed he had attacked and killed them. He showed a musket barrel and several pieces of iron as proof.
- They may have split into two groups, one traveling north toward the Chesapeake Bay and the other south to Croatoan Island. This is what most researchers now think happened.

What do you think?

High Hopes

Ralph Lane, a member of Raleigh's Roanoke Colony, wrote these words about Virginia:

> We have discovered . . . the goodliest soil under the cope of heaven, so abounding with sweet trees, that bring such sundry rich and pleasant gums, grapes of such greatness, as France, Spain, nor Italy have no greater. . . . The continent is of huge and unknown greatness, and very well peopled and towned, though savagely, and the climate so wholesome, that we not one sick since we landed there.

Accounts like these encouraged many people to venture across the Atlantic. They went with high hopes—but when they had to deal with the New World and its inhabitants on a practical day-to-day basis, their hopes were often disappointed. Their new home was not the earthly paradise they expected, and the "savages" who lived there seemed strange and frightening.

Building Jamestown

Three
THE VIRGINIA COMPANY
AND THE ORIGINS OF THE JAMESTOWN SETTLEMENT

Between Jamestown Island and mainland Virginia, the James River runs in a deep and narrow channel. The water is deep enough so the colonists could sail their ships close to the island and tie them to the trees. The channel is narrow enough that if Spanish ships tried to attack the colony they would have to come within weapons range.

One hundred and eight colonists made the voyage from England this time. They were given a detailed list of instructions about how to find a good location for a colony and what to do when they found it. They were told to look for gold and a trading route to the Far East. Jamestown Island, sixty miles inland from the Chesapeake Bay, must have looked like the perfect place. "When it shall please God to send you on the coast of Virginia," the instructions read, "you shall do your best endeavour to find out a safe port in the entrance of some navigable river, making choice of such a one as runneth farthest into the land."

Jamestown today, aerial view

The settlers had been sent by the Virginia Company to set up a colony in the New World. The Virginia Company was a joint stock company, which meant that many investors had given money to finance the expedition. In return for their support, the investors would get part of the profit from the gold and trade they hoped the colony would bring. No one expected the colonists would stay for very long; they just wanted to set up a base and get rich quickly.

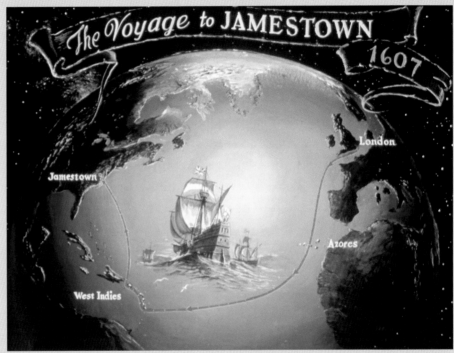

Voyage to Jamestown

England's King James I granted the Virginia Company a **charter**, giving them permission to establish a colony in the New World. Although King James probably did not realize it, this charter was one of the most important documents of early American history. The charter gave the colonists the same rights and freedoms as they would have had back in England. Usually, colonists were completely under the control of the company that financed them. In this case, however, they were technically still governed by

*A **charter** is a grant of rights, franchises, or privileges by the sovereign power of a state or country.*

the king and the laws of England. The king was thousands of miles away, though, and this allowed the colonists more opportunities to rule themselves. The differences might have been small to the original colonists, but this charter opened the door to greater freedoms in the future.

In April of 1607, after four months at sea, the colonists reached the coast of Virginia and began to look for a colony site. On May 14, they came to Jamestown Island and went ashore. It must have felt wonderful to be finally off the ship for good. As they stood on the shore of their new home with the warm spring air on their faces, they were probably excited about the future and eager to start building their new homes.

Life was not easy for the Jamestown colonists. Very soon after they arrived in the New World, they were attacked by some of the Native people. The colonists fought them off, and over the next few weeks, they built a fort with high wooden walls around their settlement. The fort was in the shape of a triangle, with the storehouse, church, and houses inside its walls.

Some of the colonists tried hard to help the colony thrive. They worked to make sure the settlement had plenty of food. Others, however, were more interested in the gold they had heard could be found in the New World. Although this was one of the reasons the colonists had been sent to Virginia, there was no gold to be found in the area. The men who spent their time gold-hunting did not contribute a lot to the survival of the community.

John Smith, one of the seven men the Virginia Company had chosen to help govern the new colony, was frustrated by the way the other members of the council were running the settlement. The Virginia Company kept pressuring the colonists to send shipments of valuable New World goods back to Europe. Some colonists, not used to the hard work of surviving in the wilderness, tried to run away and find a

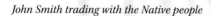

John Smith trading with the Native people

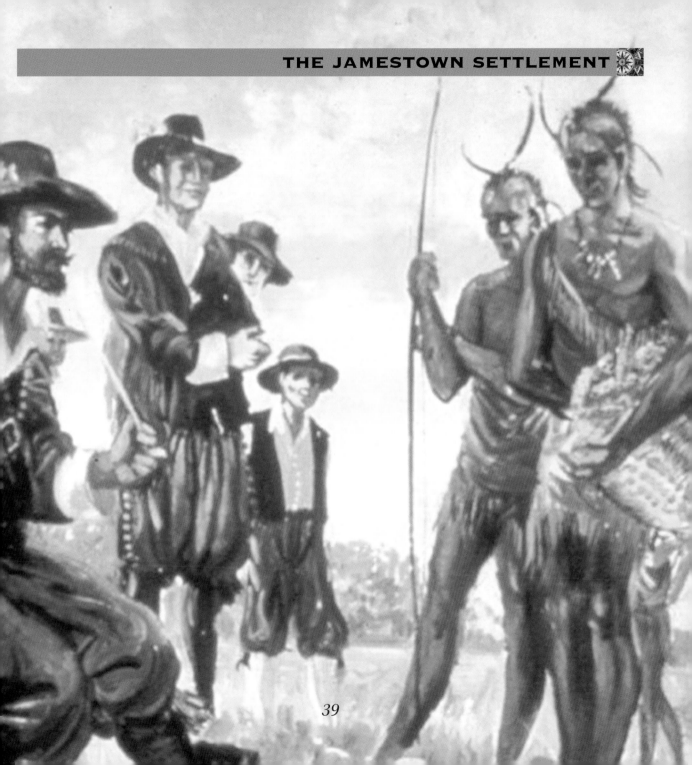

Pocahontas statue

40

ship to take them home to England. Most of the people did not worry enough about making sure they would have enough food for the winter.

A few months after arriving on Jamestown Island, Smith left to explore the area and find food. During this time, he was captured by Powhatan, the chief of the local Indian tribe. Later in his life, Smith told the story of how Powhatan had intended to execute him. He was saved, he said, when the chief's twelve-year-old daughter Pocahontas intervened.

The story of Pocahontas is one of the most famous stories to come out of this time. Her real name was Matoaka, but her people fondly called her Pocahontas, which means "playful." Because John Smith often bragged and exaggerated his own importance, we are not sure how true his story about his rescue by Pocahontas really was. Some writers think Smith made the story up after Pocahontas's death to make himself look important, since she had become famous. Other people think the story was true but that Smith misinterpreted what had happened. They believe that the "execution" was part of a ritual adopting Smith into the tribe. Whatever the truth, Pocahontas did become an important figure in the lives of the Jamestown colonists.

John Smith spent about four weeks with Powhatan's tribe, and when they released him, he left as a friend. In January of 1608, Smith returned to Jamestown and discovered that conditions in the colony had gotten much worse. People were unhappy, there was not enough food, and they wanted to go home. Smith helped the colonists establish trade with the Indians, and they were able to get enough food in this way to make it through the rest of the winter.

Most of the Jamestown settlers probably met Pocahontas for the first time shortly after this, when Powhatan sent her to ask for the release of his people taken captive by the colonists. For the next several years, she was a familiar figure around the colony and, for a time, an uneasy peace existed between the Indians and the English settlers. Pocahontas carried messages to the colony from her father and came with Indians bringing food and furs to trade for the iron tools of the Europeans.

In September of 1608, the settlers elected John Smith president of the governing council. As president, Smith had the authority to run the colony as he thought it should be run. He increased the colony's defenses, started farms, and made sure that all the colonists worked at farming. His motto was "He who does not work, will not eat."

Jamestown began to flourish under Smith's leadership and with the help of trade from the Native people. Unfortunately, late in 1609, two events happened that seriously hurt the growing community. In October, Smith was hurt when a bag of gunpowder exploded; he had to go back to England. Then, just before winter, a ship arrived with four hundred new colonists.

The colony might have had enough provisions if it had not been for the new arrivals. Pocahontas did her best to provide some food,

but it was not enough. The winter of 1609–1610 became known as the "starving time"; only 60 of 504 colonists survived.

In the spring, the hungry, miserable colonists wanted nothing more than to go back to England. They abandoned the Jamestown settlement and got on a ship to go home. However, they had made it only to the mouth of the James

Re-creation of the settlers' ship

River, sixty miles away, when they encountered another ship. This ship, sent by the Virginia Company, was headed for Jamestown carrying supplies and a new governor, Lord De La Warr. De La Warr insisted on continuing on to Jamestown, taking the colonists back with him.

De La Warr was a harsh man, and he ruled the colony as if it were a military encampment. He also did nothing to encourage good relations with the Native

43

Native Americans knew how to harvest the land

Americans in the area. During the long, hard winter before De La Warr's arrival, the desperate settlers had resorted to raiding Indian villages for food. Now, De La Warr, with much less of an excuse, continued the raids, also burning the Indian's houses and fields. This conflict was called the First Angelo-Powhatan War.

After De La Warr became governor of Jamestown, Pocahontas stopped visiting the town almost completely. In 1610, she married an Indian named Kocoum and went to live along the Potomac, nearly a hundred miles to the north of the English colony. One of the colonists, Captain Samuel Argall, however, discovered where she was living and kidnapped her. Argall sent a message to Powhatan, saying he would let her go in exchange for the release of the English prisoners and weapons the Indians had taken, as well as some corn. Powhatan paid only part of the ransom and asked that they treat his daughter well.

Argall took Pocahontas back to Jamestown

An American Indian demonstrates Native cooking

45

with him, and she went to live in the nearby settlement of Henrico. While she was living in Henrico, she converted to Christianity and met John Rolfe. Rolfe had come to Virginia in 1609 with his wife, but his wife died not long after they had arrived there.

In 1614, nearly a year after she had been captured, Sir Thomas Dale, governor of Henrico, took Pocahontas and 150 of his own men to get the rest of the ransom from Powhatan. Before Dale and his group reached Powhatan, however, they were attacked by Indians. Dale's reaction was to burn Native villages and kill several Indian men. In the middle of this, Pocahontas managed to find two of her brothers, who took her back to Powhatan.

Powhatan was probably happy to see his favorite daughter again. He would have been glad to discover that she was doing well among the white settlers. Pocahontas told her father she had fallen in love with John Rolfe and wanted to marry him. Powhatan gave his blessing to the marriage and let his daughter return to the English settlements.

Having been baptized into the Church of England with the name Rebecca, Pocahontas married John Rolfe on April 5, 1614. The marriage of Pocahontas and John Rolfe was a good thing for both the English and the Native Americans. Powhatan called it a "peace-making

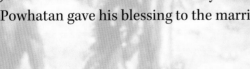

Trading with the Indians

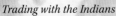

marriage" and sent Pocahontas's uncle and two of her brothers to represent him at the wedding. The marriage marked the end of the First Anglo-Powhatan War. It was probably the first interracial marriage in Virginia.

Two years later, in 1616, Pocahontas traveled to England with John Rolfe and their son Thomas. The governor, Sir Thomas Dale, made

Romanticize *means to treat as if ideal or heroic.*

Tuberculosis *is a disease affecting the lungs that is characterized by toxic or allergic symptoms.*

the voyage to raise money for the Virginia Company, and he took Pocahontas along to attract public interest. While in England, Pocahontas met King James and many of the rich and famous families of London society. Everybody liked the twenty-two-year-old Pocahontas, and because of her, the English began to **romanticize** Native American society—about which they really knew very little—originating the idea of the "noble savage."

After seven months in England, Pocahontas and John Rolfe prepared to return to Virginia. They set sail but Pocahontas was very sick, possibly with pneumonia or **tuberculosis**, and Rolfe had to

Jamestown 1641

Instructions for the Virginia Colony

Here are some of the instructions that the Virginia Company sent with the first group of colonists in 1606:

When it shall please God to send you on the coast of Virginia, you shall do your best endeavour to find out a safe port in the entrance of some navigable river, making choice of such a one as runneth farthest into the land, and if you happen to discover divers portable rivers, and amongst them any one that hath two main branches, if the difference be not great, make choice of that which bendeth most toward the North-West for that way you shall soonest find the other sea. . . .

You must observe if you can, whether the river on which you plant doth spring out of mountains or out of lakes. If it be out of any lake, the passage to the other sea will be more easy, and [it] is like enough, that out of the same lake you shall find some spring which run[s] the contrary way towards the East India Sea. . . .

You must take especial care that you choose a seat for habitation that shall not be over burthened with woods near your town; for all the men you have, shall not be able to cleanse twenty acres a year; besides that it may serve for a covert for your enemies round about.

Neither must you plant in a low or moist place, because it will prove unhealthfull. You shall judge of the good air by the people; for some part of that coast where the lands are low, have their people blear eyed, and with swollen bellies and legs; but if the naturals [natives] be strong and clean made, it is a true sign of a wholesome soil. . . .

Lastly and chiefly the way to prosper and achieve good success is to make yourselves all of one mind for the good of your country and your own, and to serve and fear God the Giver of all Goodness, for every plantation which our Heavenly Father hath not planted shall be rooted out.

take her ashore before they actually got away from England. The doctors did everything they could, but Pocahontas was too sick and she died. Rolfe buried her in the churchyard at Gravesend, England, left their son with a guardian, and went back to Virginia.

Even though Pocahontas lived only twenty-two years, she had a huge impact on the lives of the English settlers in Virginia, and she has become a famous, romantic character in American history. She helped make trade possible between her tribe and the colonists, and she acted

John Smith, the Adventurer

John Smith lives in history's stories because in real life he seemed to be truly a bit larger than life.

When he was a young man, he fought against the Turks in Hungary; after beheading three Turks in a single afternoon, a grateful Hungarian prince granted him a coat of arms with three Turks' heads emblazoned on it. The Latin motto on the coat of arms meant, "Vanquish and live." John Smith didn't always vanquish his enemies, but he did manage to stay alive. When the Turks took him captive, Smith eventually escaped and spent the next several years wandering through Russia, Poland, Germany, and North Africa, fighting pirates and having numerous other adventures. When he finally made his way back home, life in England must have seemed tame to him; no wonder he persuaded the merchants who were organizing the expedition to Virginia to hire him on.

After his return from Jamestown in 1609, Smith again sailed across the Atlantic two more times. In 1614, he mapped the coastline of the region he named New England, and the following year, he sailed again. This time, though, pirates captured him. By the time he escaped three months later, he had lost everything. Penniless, he returned to England, and never traveled to North America again. However, for the rest of his life, he wrote and talked about the lands across the ocean.

as a go-between in Indian-English relations. Her marriage to John Rolfe brought an end to the fighting between the Indians and the English and the peace lasted for years after her death. The little Indian girl who brought food to help the inexperienced English colonists survive has been a well-known American story for almost four centuries, and her story will likely continue to be told for centuries more.

These are the Lines that shew thy Face but those
That shew thy Grace and Glory, brighter bee
Thy Faire-Discoueries and Fowle-Overthrowes
Of Salvages, much Civiliz'd by thee
Best shew thy Spirit and to it Glory Wyn;
So, thou art Brasse without, but Golde within.

A memorial to John Smith stands on the shore of Jamestown's site

Jamestown settlers began to plant tobacco

Four
JAMESTOWN CONTINUES TO GROW

The large, broad leaves of the tobacco plant have meant many different things to different cultures throughout history. For Native American tribes, tobacco was a sacred plant, given to them by their god and used in religious ceremonies. For a lot of people today, tobacco means lung cancer, nicotine patches, and antismoking campaigns. For the Jamestown colonists, however, tobacco meant life itself.

Before the English settlers in Virginia discovered they could grow tobacco, their colony was struggling to survive. John Rolfe was the one who introduced tobacco to the Jamestown colony, making him famous for more than just being Pocahontas's husband.

In 1609, on his way to Virginia for the first time, Rolfe had purchased some tobacco seeds when his ship stopped in the Caribbean. After he settled near Jamestown, Rolfe started experimenting with the Caribbean tobacco seeds, crossing it with the native tobacco to produce a new variety. In 1613, Rolfe gave some of his tobacco to his friends to try. They liked it, so he sent the rest of his crop to England to be sold there.

James Fort homes (re-creation)

The English settlers gathered the native plants for study.

The next year, Rolfe married Pocahontas, which stopped the war between the Indians and the settlers. The new peace allowed the colonists to focus more of their time and resources on expanding their colony. The colonists began to grow Rolfe's new tobacco, which was becoming quite popular in England.

The rising popularity of tobacco had an amazing impact on the society of colonial Virginia. Colonists wanted more land so they could grow more tobacco. For a while, they even grew tobacco along the streets of Jamestown. More land, in the form of huge plantations, meant they could grow more crops. More land and more crops meant they needed more people to care for the tobacco plants and harvest them.

Many of the common English people were now beginning to see Virginia as a place where they could make their fortunes growing tobacco. Unfortunately for them, it was very expensive to travel to the New World. The Virginia Company came up with a solution to this problem in the form of indentured servitude. The Virginia Company would pay for the voyage for an immigrant, and the immigrant would then agree to pay them back with several years of labor in the New World. This method of getting to the colonies became very common. Over the next several decades, hundreds of thousands of indentured servants—mostly unmarried men in their late teens or early twenties—arrived in Virginia.

In 1619, another event occurred that changed the face of America forever. A Dutch ship, traveling in the Chesapeake Bay, took twenty Africans to Jamestown and traded them for food. These first Africans were treated as indentured servants. Once they worked a certain number of years, they were free and could purchase their own land or do what they liked. This event, however, led eventually to the system of slave labor in America.

Slavery began slowly in the American colonies. After the first twenty, only three hundred more Africans arrived in Virginia over the next thirty years. These were still considered indentured servants, with all the rights of the English indentured servants. But within twenty-one years after that, there were two thousand Africans, and by the Revolutionary War just over a century later, there were half a million. Sometime during the second half of the seventeenth century, the colonists passed laws that made a distinction between white and black servants. After that, slavery became an established system, with thousands of African slaves working on plantations all across the southeastern part of America.

Voting booth

56

Even with the introduction of tobacco in Virginia—with vast plantations and indentured servants to work them—life was not easy for the colonists. They were no longer starving and tobacco had brought them plenty of money, but they had to face other problems. For one thing, diseases were very common. In the first twenty years that the colony existed, eight thousand colonists arrived from England, but only twelve hundred of them survived.

Although some died of starvation in the early years—especially the "starving time" winter of 1609–1610—and some were killed in conflicts with Indians, most died from disease. The northern colonies in New England did not have the same ongoing problem with disease *epidemics* as the southern colonies because of the colder climate.

Epidemics are outbreaks (as of disease) of sudden and quick spread, growth, or development.

Burial of the dead

Jamestown foundations today

Another problem the Jamestown colony faced was that there were many more men than women in the settlement. Powhatan, the Indian chief, seeing how few women there were in the English colony, hoped that the colonists would soon become dependent on him, since they had hardly anyone to do the "women's work" of growing and preparing food.

Recruiting means trying to secure the services of someone.

Indentured means contracted to work for a specified time in exchange for travel expenses, room, and board.

Powhatan's hopes were not fulfilled, but the lack of women did present the colony with an unusual set of struggles. Many of the men were forced to help with cooking and cleaning, sewing and washing clothes. Today, men often work with women to do these jobs, but at the time, these were things generally done only by women.

The Virginia Company tried to do something about the shortage of women colonists by *recruiting* upper-class English women to travel to the Jamestown colony. The men of the colony could pay the Virginia Company to find potential wives and send them across the Atlantic Ocean. One hundred and forty-seven English women came to Jamestown in this way, but there were still far more men than women. The huge numbers of men arriving as *indentured* servants did nothing to help this, and it was many years before the balance of

Guards at Jamestown's (re-creation)

Typical Jamestown house

men and women evened out.

As the Jamestown colony grew and smaller settlements sprang up around it, the colonists began to be unhappy with the governors the Virginia Company sent them—many of whom were violent and harsh men. The governors had been given complete control, and the colonists wanted to have something to say about the laws that governed them. In 1619, the Virginia Company agreed to create a legislative assembly. This legislative assembly, called the House of Burgesses, was the first representative legislature in the New World. This meant that, for the first time, representatives of the people would be able to help make their own laws.

On July 30, 1619, the House of Burgesses met for the first time in the Jamestown church, because it was "the most convenient place . . . they could finde to sitt in." The assembly was made up of twenty-two men: the governor, his council, and the burgesses (representatives) from all the larger plantations. They met for six days in the hot, stuffy church. The heat and humidity were so bad that one of the men even died.

The House of Burgesses was important because it became a pattern that other American colonies would follow. The Virginia assembly itself lasted only four years, however. In 1624, King James I got suspicious of the House of Burgesses. He was afraid that the colonists would rebel and that he would lose control of the colony. King James cancelled the charter he had granted the Virginia Company, which gave them the right to govern the Jamestown colony. He made Virginia a royal colony, putting it directly under his power.

Although the colonists lost their right to represent themselves in the House of Burgesses when King James took back control from the Virginia Company, in some ways this was a good thing. The owners of the Virginia Company had started fighting with each other about how to run the company, and, as a result, the company

Conflict between Natives and English settlers

Burning of the James Fort

was almost bankrupt. The Jamestown colony was able to better grow and thrive under the control of the king than it had been under the control of the Virginia Company.

One of the reasons King James gave for putting Virginia under his direct control was the Indian massacre that took place in 1622. Powhatan had died in 1618, and his brother Opechancanough had become chief. Opechancanough saw how the white settlers were spreading out into his territory and realized, as Powhatan had not, the danger to the Indian way of life.

Opechancanough planned to attack both the fort at Jamestown and the settlements that had grown up around the original colony. He wanted to make the English leave and never come back.

Jamestown itself was saved by an Indian boy who had spent time among the colonists and converted to Christianity. The boy warned the settlers of the Indian attack, but it was too late to send the message to the people living on plantations along the river. Three hundred and forty-seven settlers died when the Powhatans struck. The shocked colonists barricaded themselves inside the Jamestown fort to protect themselves from more attacks. As part of their assault, the Indians had also burned the plantations, live-stock, and crops. Without the crops the English had counted on to get through the winter, food ran short and over four hundred died of malnutrition and disease.

When news of the massacre arrived in England the next sum-mer, the Virginia Company and King James sent supplies and weapons and called on the colonists to take revenge. The colonists followed this advice to an extreme, slaughtering Indians and burning their villages.

In 1644, the colonists fought the Second Anglo-Powhatan War. The Indians lost, and in 1646, they signed a peace treaty that ban-ished them from the Chesapeake Bay area, the land they had lived on for generations before the arrival of the white settlers.

When the colonists had first arrived in Virginia in 1606, they were inexperienced and almost unable to meet their own needs. Without the help of the Indians, they would not have been able to survive. Forty years later, however, the Jamestown settlers had gotten used to living without the luxuries of English society. They had expanded their colony to include numerous smaller settle-ments and large tobacco plantations. They no longer needed help from the Native people. They only wanted their land.

In 1652, a *civil war* in England removed the king from power. *Parliament* took control of England and its colonies until 1660, when King Charles II was restored to the throne. During this time of parliamentary control, Virginia governed itself almost com-

Civil war is a war between opposing groups of the same nation.

Parliament is the supreme legislative body of England.

Laws for Cleanliness

Because of the problems with disease, the early governors of Jamestown made laws to try and keep the town as clean as possible:

There shall no man or woman, Launderer or Launderesse, dare to wash any un-cleane Linnen, drive bucks, or throw out the water or suds of fowle cloathes, in the open streete, within the Pallizadoes, or within forty foote of the same, nor rench, and make cleane, any kettle, pot, or pan, or such like vessell within twenty foote of the olde well, or new Pumpe.

House of Burgess

In the summer of 1619, the assembly:

- made laws against drunkenness, idleness, and gambling.
- talked about protecting themselves from the Indians.
- talked about baptizing the Indians.
- passed a law that would require people to go to church regularly.
- put a servant on trial for improper conduct.

65

Tobacco—a Plant That Changed History

American Indians considered tobacco to be a sacred plant, given to them by God. They used it in ceremonies with care and reverence. White people, however, looked at tobacco as a way to get rich. Many white men had discovered that they liked smoking—and for them, it was not a spiritual experience but simply a pleasure to be enjoyed as often as possible. Huge tobacco plantations needed many workers—and eventually, plantation owners came to look at black-skinned workers as less than human. Today, we know that tobacco contains chemicals that are addictive—and even worse, that it causes lung cancer. This once-sacred and divine gift to humanity has been abused and over-used—and it has left behind a legacy of death, disease, and injustice.

The first Englishmen to encounter tobacco, however, believed it to be a medicinal herb. Thomas Hariot, a member of the first unsuccessful colony at Roanoke, wrote these words about tobacco:

There is an herb which is sowed apart by itself . . . the Spaniards generally call it Tabacco. The leaves thereof being dried and brought into powder, they use to take the smoke thereof, by sucking it through pipes made of clay, into their stomach and head; from whence it . . . opens all the pores and passages of the body . . . whereby their bodies are notably preserved in health, and know not many grievous diseases. . . .

pletely. Outwardly, the colonists stayed loyal to the king during this time, but little by little they were getting used to making their own rules. Virginia society was beginning to stabilize. Indian attacks were not the threat they had been. There was generally enough food. Tobacco had brought prosperity, and the colony was no longer a wilderness outpost.

Tobacco today

A LAW
OF
MARYLAND
Concerning
RELIGION.

Oras much as in a well-governed and Christian Commonwealth, Matters concerning Religion and the Honour of God ought to be in the fir place to be taken into serious consideration, and endeavoured to be settled. Be it therefore Ordained and Enacted by the Right Honourab CÆCILIUS Lord Baron of *Baltemore*, absolute Lord and Proprietary of this Province, with the Advice and Consent of the Upper an Lower House of this General Assembly, That whatsoever person or persons within this Province and the Islands thereunto belonging, sha from henceforth blaspheme GOD, that is curse him ; or shall deny our Saviour JESUS CHRIST to be the Son of God, or shall deny the Holy Trinity, the Father, Son, & Holy Ghost; or the Godhead of any of the said Three Persons of the Trinity, or the Unity of the Godhead or shall use or utter any reproachful speeches, words, or language, concerning the Holy Trinity, or any of the said three Persons thereof, shall be pu nished with death, and confiscation or forfeiture of all his or her Lands and Goods to the Lord Proprietary and his Heirs.

Oras much as in a well-governed and Christian
pla e to be taken into serious consideration, and endeavo
CÆCILIUS Lord Baron of *Baltemore*, absolute Lord a
Lower House of this General Assembly, That whatsoever
from henceforth blaspheme GOD, that is curse him ; or
the Holy Trinity, the Father, Son, & Holy Ghost; or the
shall use or utter any

Five
MARYLAND, THE CAROLINAS, AND GEORGIA

Today, everyone in America has the freedom to belong to whatever church or religion they want. People can follow their own beliefs, and it is against the law to discriminate against them because of it. At the time when the American colonies were founded, however, people cared a great deal which religion someone belonged to. In the 1500s, England had left the Roman Catholic Church and formed the Church of England. Most people in England, and in England's New World colonies, belonged to the Church of England. In fact, people who belonged to other churches were not allowed to work at certain high-level jobs.

A man named George Calvert lived in England in the early 1600s. Calvert was active in English politics, and in 1617, the king even knighted him for the work he had done. In 1625, Calvert became a Roman Catholic and was forced to resign from his political positions. The king really liked Calvert, however, and so he made him the First Baron of Baltimore, a town on the coast of Ireland. As Lord Baltimore, Calvert had land and an income to support himself and his family.

Calvert was restless living in Ireland. He had heard the stories about England's colonies and he wanted to try founding a colony of his own. With a grant from King Charles, Calvert established a colony on the coast of Newfoundland in 1628. For almost two years, he lived in the colony he named Prince of Avalon, but French ships frequently raided their supplies and his wife complained that the climate was too harsh. In 1629, Calvert decided to move to the Virginia colonies.

Calvert had been a part of the original Virginia Company that had been responsible for the founding of Jamestown. Now, however, he found he was unwelcome. Calvert was a Roman Catholic, and the governing council refused to allow him and his family to settle in the area.

When Calvert talked to King Charles about what had happened, the king promised to give him a large piece of land to the north of Virginia. The king named the area Maryland after the queen, Henrietta Maria. Calvert had two dreams for this colony. First, he wanted a place where he would be completely in charge; he wanted the power and money this would give him. Second, he wanted to establish a place where Roman Catholics could live and not be persecuted for their faith.

Before King Charles actually granted him the charter to the land, however, Calvert died in 1632. The king granted the charter anyhow, giving it to Calvert's oldest son, Cecil. Cecil Calvert became the second Lord Baltimore and founded the colony of Maryland in 1634.

The charter gave Lord Baltimore almost as much power as a

The Vatican, the center of Catholicism

John Calvin

John Calvin was an important religious reformer. He believed that Christians should follow a strict moral code, and he taught that the Bible should be interpreted as literal (rather than spiritual or symbolic) truth. Calvin also believed that some people were "predestined" for salvation, while others were not. In other words, God chose some people—the "elect"—to be saved, while others were condemned to hell. According to Calvin, human free will played no role in eternal salvation. Calvin's influence on American attitudes and ideas can still be seen.

John Calvin

king in the new colony. He was required to send King Charles a small tribute every year—two Indian arrows and one-fifth of any gold and silver mined—but he had almost complete authority in the running of the colony. When new colonists arrived in Maryland, Lord Baltimore gave them either large estates or else tiny farms on these estates. Like the *serfs* who worked the land for the *feudal* lords of the Middle Ages, those on the smaller farms were required to pay rent to those who owned the land. Lord Baltimore gave most of the land and power to his Catholic friends and relatives.

England was a Protestant nation, though, and, since Maryland was an English colony, Lord Baltimore could not keep Protestants from settling there. As a result, Maryland had the most freedom of religion of all the early American colonies. Many Puritans came to Maryland from Virginia to settle because of its religious *tolerance*. The Puritans also colonized much of New England. Although Puritans were Protestant, they did not belong to the Church of England, but to a stricter, Calvinist church. They were often *discriminated* against in England and in some of the English colonies.

The large numbers of Puritans and other Protestants arriving in Maryland exceeded the number of Catholics by a great deal. The Catholics, although they were in charge of the colony's government, started to worry that they would soon be pushed out of the way and discriminated against as they had been in England.

In 1649, the Toleration Act was passed, guaranteeing equal legal rights to people from all Christian groups. At the time, the Toleration Act was a great step toward religious freedom, although

Serfs were people of a subservient class of a feudal system who were bound to the land and the will of the lord.

Feudal means characteristic of a system of political organization where tenants served the lord of the land.

Tolerance means acceptance of differences.

Discriminated means treated differently because of religion, race, gender, or some other characteristic.

Peasants *are people who till the soil as small landowners or laborers.*

Aristocrats *are people of a governing body or upper class made up of hereditary nobility.*

John Locke

Maryland residents were still expected to believe in the Trinity and not to insult the Virgin Mary or the Apostles.

With the Toleration Act in place, the Catholics who had founded the colony felt more secure. It was now illegal for the large numbers of Protestants to discriminate against them.

Just as King Charles granted Lord Baltimore most of the rights of a king over the people of Maryland, in 1663, he also gave the land that now makes up North and South Carolina and Georgia to eight lords who were his close friends and supporters. These lords, called the Lord Proprietors, had the same kingly powers as Lord Baltimore. King Charles gave his friends this land because he wanted to expand and strengthen England's colonies in America. France and Spain were still in control of large parts of the New World, and England wanted to build up its own power there.

The philosopher John Locke wrote a plan called the Grand Model. The Grand Model described how the land owned by the Lord Proprietors would be governed. The Lord Proprietors would divide the land into counties, and each county would have an earl and two barons. Tenants would farm the land, under the control of the lords of their county.

The land was a wild tangle of swamps and dense forests, however, and John Locke had designed the Grand Model for a more cultivated country of meadows and farmland. The Lord Proprietors never were able to carry out their ambitious plan of transforming the southern American colonies into a place of ***peasants*** and ***aristocrats*** such as England had outgrown hundreds of years before.

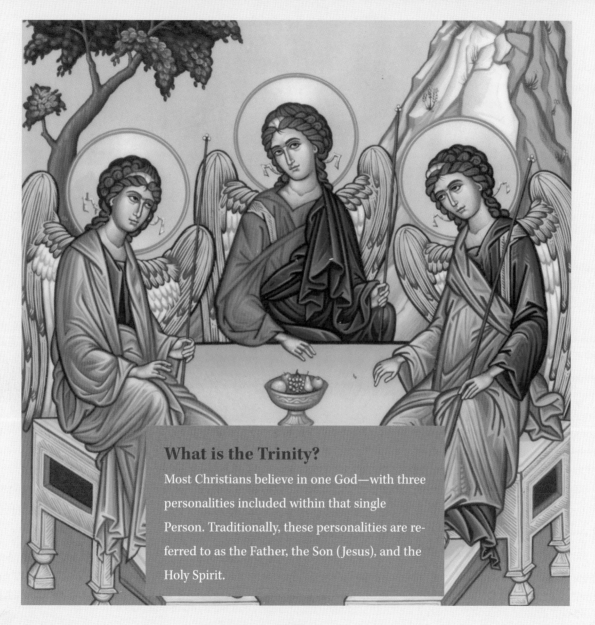

What is the Trinity?

Most Christians believe in one God—with three personalities included within that single Person. Traditionally, these personalities are referred to as the Father, the Son (Jesus), and the Holy Spirit.

An early portrayal of slavery

Not until seven years later, in 1670, did the first settlers establish a colony in the Carolinas. These settlers arrived from Barbados, an island in the West Indies controlled by the English. Huge sugar plantations covered the island of Barbados, worked by slaves brought in from Africa. People earned fortunes growing the bamboo-like sugarcane, and ships arrived from England regularly, carrying hundreds of passengers eager to get rich. Before long, however, a small number of "sugar barons" had bought up most of the land and newcomers had nowhere to plant their own crops. Still hopeful of becoming rich, several hundred of these English immigrants traveled to the coast of the Carolinas and built a town along the banks of the Ashley River. The original colony disappeared long ago, but several years after arriving in North America, the settlers moved to a nearby site, where Charleston, South Carolina, is still located today.

When the settlers sailed from Barbados, they brought their black slaves with them. In this way, the slave trade in South Carolina began at the same time as the colony, unlike most of the other colonies. In fact, not only did the colonists bring in African slaves, but they also sold local Native Americans as slaves to the West Indies and to the northern colonies.

Slavery

Whereas the Virginia colonists grew tobacco and those in Barbados grew sugarcane, the moneymaking crop in South Carolina became rice. Although rice grew wild in the area, the set-

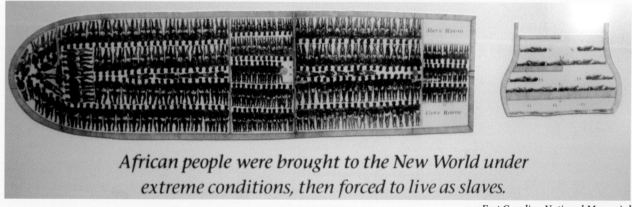

African people were brought to the New World under extreme conditions, then forced to live as slaves.

Fort Caroline National Memorial

tlers preferred the taste of a type of rice they imported from Madagascar in Africa. The huge swamps along the coast of South Carolina were ideal for raising rice, which needed wet, marshy ground to grow. Unfortunately, swarms of mosquitoes also lived in the swamps, and people tending the rice plants faced the danger of malaria and other tropical diseases.

None of the white workers could survive for very long in the rice fields, so the plantation owners used African slaves almost exclusively. Many of the slaves had worked with rice in Africa and knew how to take care of it. They were also slightly more immune to malaria, although huge numbers of them still died. The plantation owners discovered that it was cheaper to continually buy more slaves to replace the ones who died than to properly care for the slaves they already owned. The constant demand for more workers fueled the slave trade for years to come.

North Carolina, even though it was officially part of South Carolina until the early 1700s, was a very different place than its southern half.

The owners of the South Carolina rice plantations were wealthy and aristocratic men. North Carolina, on the other hand, was mainly settled by people who were unhappy with the religious discrimination or rich landowners in South Carolina and Virginia. Since the North Carolina settlers were usually small farmers or hunters who lived off the land, large towns and coastal trade did not develop as it did in other colonies. As a result, North Carolina was generally a more independent and down-to-earth place. The people were considered some of the most democratic minded in the American colonies. Despite this trait, the colonists treated the local Indians no differently than did the other white settlers. Before too many years had passed, the settlers had killed or driven out almost all the coastal Native Americans tribes.

The last of the original thirteen colonies settled by England was Georgia. James Oglethorpe, one of the founders of the colony, was a respected member of English government. When one of his close friends died in a debtor's prison, Oglethorpe began investigating the conditions in these prisons. What he found horrified him. The prisons were damp, filthy, and overcrowded. He came up with a plan to take debtors to the New World instead of imprisoning them.

The English government had again become nervous about the Spanish in Florida and the French in Louisiana. A colony established in the southern part of English land in America would be a buffer between these foreign-held colonies to the south and the prosperous English colonies to the north. Oglethorpe's colony for debtors would solve two problems at once for the English government.

In 1732, King George II granted a group of trustees a charter to establish the proposed colony. The area was named Georgia after the king. The trustees would govern the new colony for twenty-one years, and then the king would take back control. While the trustees were in charge, they had total control; the settlers had no say in the governing of the colony, but they did receive land without having to pay rent for ten years.

Since many of the colonists were to be debtors with no money of their own, England helped fund the colony. Georgia was the only English colony helped in this way. Slavery and alcoholic drinks were illegal in the new colony—another way Georgia was different

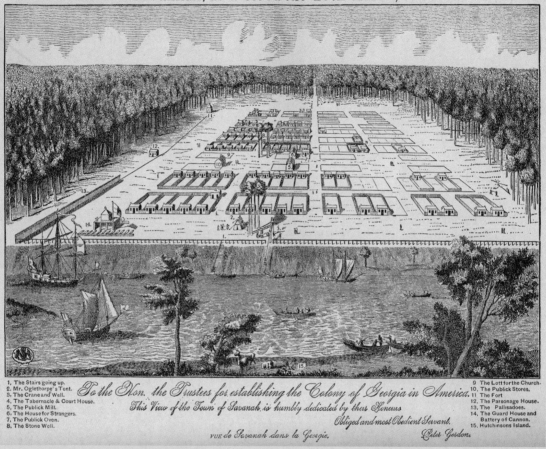

View of Savannah, as it stood the 29th March, A. D. 1734.

1, The Stairs going up.
2, Mr. Oglethorpe's Tent.
3, The Crane and Well.
4, The Tabernacle & Court House.
5, The Publick Mill.
6, The House for Strangers.
7, The Publick Oven.
8, The Stone Well.

9 The Lott for the Church.
10, The Publick Stores,
11, The Fort
12, The Parsonage House,
13, The Pallisadoes.
14, The Guard House and Battery of Cannon.
15, Hutchinsons Island.

To the Hon. the Trustees for establishing the Colony of Georgia in America.

This View of the Town of Savanah is humbly dedicated by their Honours

Obliged and most Obedient Servant,

Peter Gordon

VUE de Savanah dans la Georgie.

from the other colonies at its beginning.

In February of 1733, James Oglethorpe and thirty-five families arrived in Georgia and began the founding of the city of Savannah. Oglethorpe served as governor of Georgia for twelve years before moving back to England. In that time and for a number of years afterward, the colony grew very slowly.

Although Georgia had been founded as a place for debtors, Oglethorpe's plan did not succeed. Most of the debtors decided they would rather face prison than risk the difficulties of pioneer life. Records show that only eleven families of debtors were brought to settle in Georgia during its early years.

Some of the people who came to Georgia were trying to get away from religious discrimination and persecution in Europe. The Salzburgers and the Scottish Highlanders were two of these religious groups that chose to settle in Georgia. Oglethorpe gave equal legal rights to people of all Christian religious groups, except for Roman Catholics.

Georgia also attracted several *missionaries*. John and Charles Wesley and George Whitfield all spent time in Georgia soon after its founding. John Wesley, who later started the Methodist movement in England, arrived in Savannah in 1735, hoping to preach to the Native Americans. He found the colony in a disorganized state, and Oglethorpe convinced him to instead serve as a preacher to the English settlers.

At this point, Wesley had not yet experienced the defining moment of his life that started him on the road to developing the Methodist Church. He was a minister of the Church of England, and he insisted on following the formal style of High Church Anglicanism. The Georgia colonists were a diverse group, varying from the deeply religious to the criminal, but almost none of them were pleased with Wesley. The settlers were common people, making their way in a wild new country, and they had no patience with Wesley's stuffiness. When Wesley went back to England after less than three years, they were relieved to see him go.

Many who might have been interested in settling in Georgia claimed that the *prohibition* laws drove away trade, and the ban

Portrait of James Oglethorpe

Missionaries are people who seek to pass along their religious faith to nonbelievers.

Prohibition means that alcohol is illegal.

Idealistic means relating to a standard of excellence, beauty, or perfection.

against slaves kept the economy from growing. The people who did settle in Georgia were often unhappy in their new home for these same reasons. They were not pleased with the system of government that ruled them without their input. They wanted to be free to own slaves and drink liquor. They wanted to be able to purchase more land than the small lots they had been granted when they immigrated.

Before long, the colonists got their way in all these issues. First, the law against drinking was abolished. Then, in 1749, English Parliament gave in and allowed the colonists to keep slaves, although they insisted that the slaves be treated well. Finally, in 1752—almost two years before their twenty-one-year charter expired—the trustees gave control of the colony back to the king. With the king in charge, the colony started to grow more quickly. The king appointed a governor, and the colonists elected representatives to speak for them and help make the laws that governed them.

When James Oglethorpe and his ship of settlers arrived on the coast of America and started building the city of Savannah, Georgia was unique among England's other New World colonies. People called the new colony the "Charity Colony" because it was intended to be an alternative to debtor's prisons. As an experiment in charity, Georgia started out with laws quite different from those of the other colonies. Following Oglethorpe's *idealistic* vision, there was no alcohol, no slaves, and the settlers had no involvement in the making of the laws that ruled them. Twenty years after King George granted the charter for its establishment, however, Georgia looked very much like the other twelve English colonies. The English colonists were becoming Americans, with an identity of their own. They were well on their way to shaping America into the country it is today.

Another Point of View

In chapter 1, we mentioned that history is made up of many stories. The European settlers have one story to tell—but their stories intersect with others. Here is the story of Olaudah Equiano, a West African who was captured by slave traders when he was eleven:

> One day, when all our people were gone out to their work as usual, and only I and my sister were left to mind the house, two men and a woman got over our walls, and in a moment seized us both; and without giving us time to cry out or to make any resistance, they stopped our mouths and ran off with us into the nearest wood. Here they tied our hands and continued to carry us. . . . I feared I should be put to death, the white people looked and acted, as I thought, in so savage a manner; for I had never seen among any people such instances of brutal cruelty; and this is not only shown towards us blacks, but also to some of the whites themselves. . . .

Between 1526 and 1870, nearly 10 million human beings were shipped from Africa as slaves to labor in the New World. The American settlers prospered in their new home—but their success was intertwined with the tragedy of many African lives.

1584 Sir Walter Raleigh sends Philip Amadas and Arthur Barlowe to look for an ideal colony location on the North American coast. The explorers bring back enthusiastic reports about Roanoke Island, along the coast of what is now North Carolina.

August 1587 One hundred and seventeen new colonists, including women, children, and farmers, arrive in Roanoke. They discover the men Grenville left have been killed by Indians. Despite their concerns, the captain of the ship leaves them there.

1492 Christopher Columbus discovers the New World.

August 18, 1590 John White returns to the Roanoke settlement to discover the colonists have vanished, leaving the word "Croatoan" carved on a wooden palisade.

1585 Raleigh sends a group of men—mostly soldiers and scholars—to colonize Roanoke Island and explore the surrounding area.

June 11, 1578 Sir Humphrey Gilbert receives a charter from Queen Elizabeth I authorizing him to discover and colonize New World lands not already claimed by another European power.

1613 Samuel Argall kidnaps Pocahontas and sends her father, Chief Powhatan, ransom demands for her release. Powhatan refuses to pay the entire ransom, and Pocahontas remains with the European settlers.

Late Autumn 1609 Four hundred new colonists arrive in Jamestown.

1614 Sir Thomas Dale takes Pocahontas with him to get the rest of the ransom from Powhatan. After a disastrous battle, Pocahontas marries John Rolfe ending the war between the indians and settlers.

1619 The House of Burgesses, the first representative legislature in the New World, meets for the first time.

1619 A Dutch ship trades twenty Africans to the Jamestown colonists in exchange for food.

1610–1614 First Anglo-Powhatan War is caused mainly by Lord De La Warr's cruel treatment of the Indians.

Winter 1609–1610 The "starving time." A hard winter with too few provisions leaves only 60 of 504 colonists alive by spring.

May 14, 1607 Colonists sent by the Virginia Company arrive on Jamestown Island. Their mission is to find gold and a trade route across the country to the Pacific Ocean.

87

1649 The Toleration Act in Maryland gives equal legal rights to people of all Christian faiths.

1670 The first English settlement is established in the Carolinas, near what is now Charleston, South Carolina. The colonists arrive from the Barbados colony, bringing their black slaves with them.

1634 King Charles grants Calvert's oldest son, Cecil, a charter to establish a new colony, which he names Maryland.

1644–1646 Second Anglo-Powhatan War. The agreements of the peace treaty exile the Indians from their ancestral land in the Chesapeake Bay area.

1663 King Charles grants the land that now makes up North Carolina, South Carolina, and Georgia to a group of eight lords, known as the Lord Proprietors.

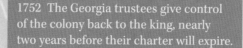
1752 The Georgia trustees give control of the colony back to the king, nearly two years before their charter will expire.

February 1733 James Oglethorpe and thirty-five families arrive in Georgia and found the city of Savannah.

1729 North Carolina is separated from South Carolina and becomes a royal colony.

1728 English member of parliament James Oglethorpe begins to campaign for prison reform and supports the idea of founding a colony for debtors in the New World.

1732 King George II grants a group of trustees a twenty-one-year charter to establish a colony in Georgia. Rules for the colony include bans on alcohol and the owning of slaves.

1749 The English government agrees to let the Georgia colonists own slaves.

THE SOUTHERN COLONIES

FURTHER READING

Alderman, Clifford Lindsay. *The Story of the Thirteen Colonies*. New York: Random House, 1966.

Barrett, Tracy. *Growing up in Colonial America*. Brookfield, Conn.: Millbrook, 1995.

Bial, Raymond. *The Powhatan*. New York: Marshall Cavendish/Benchmark, 2000.

Bosco, Peter I. *Roanoke: The Story of the Lost Colony*. Brookfield, Conn.: Millbrook, 1992.

Cornelius, James M. *The English Americans*. New York: Chelsea House, 1990.

Currie, Stephen. *Life of a Slave on a Southern Plantation*. San Diego: Lucent, 2000.

Girod, Christina M. *Georgia*. San Diego: Lucent, 2002.

Girod, Christina M. *South Carolina*. San Diego: Lucent, 2002.

Hossell, Karen Price. *Virginia*. San Diego: Lucent, 2002.

Kamensky, Jane. *The Colonial Mosaic: American Women, 1600–1760*. New York: Oxford University, 1995.

Nardo, Don. *Braving the New World, 1619–1784*. New York: Chelsea House, 1995.

Palmer, Colin A. *The First Passage: Blacks in the Americas, 1502–1617*. New York: Oxford University, 1995.

Streissguth, Thomas. *Maryland*. San Diego: Lucent, 2002.

Sullivan, George. *Pocahontas*. New York: Scholastic, 2001.

Uschan, Michael V. *North Carolina*. San Diego: Lucent, 2002.

FOR MORE INFORMATION

Georgia
www.ourgeorgiahistory.com

Jamestown
www.virtualjamestown.org

Jamestown
www.apva.org/jr.html

Roanoke
www.nps.gov/fora/roanokerev.htm

The Southern Colonies
www.kidinfo.com/American_History/
    Colonization_S_Colonies.html

Timeline of Events
www.usahistory.info/timeline

The Thirteen Original Colonies
www.timepage.org/spl/13colony.html

INDEX

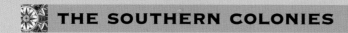

BIOGRAPHIES

AUTHOR

Sheila Nelson has always been fascinated with history and the lives of historical figures. She enjoys studying history and learning more about the events and people that have shaped our world. Sheila has written several books on history and other subjects. Recently, she completed a master's degree and now lives in Rochester, New York, with her husband and their baby daughter.

SERIES CONSULTANT

Dr. Jack N. Rakove is a professor of history and American studies at Stanford University, where he is director of American studies. The winner of the 1997 Pulitzer Prize in history, Dr. Rakove is the author of *The Unfinished Election of 2000, Constitutional Culture and Democratic Rule,* and *James Madison and the Creation of the American Republic.* He is also the president of the Society for the History of the Early American Republic.

PICTURE CREDITS